# Songs for Walt

# Songs *for* Walt

Garrett Buhl Robinson

Library of Congress Control Number: 2024919286

Poet in the Park
New York City
In Humanity I see Grace, Beauty and Dignity.

www.PoetinthePark.com

# Table of Content

—those hot, sad, wrenching times—the army volunteers, all States—or North or South—the wounded, suffering, dying—the exhausting, sweating summers, marches, battles, carnage—those trenches hurriedly heap'd by the corpse-thousands, mainly unknown—

Will the America of the future—will this vast rich Union ever realize what itself cost?

— Walt Whitman

# *Dedication*

— for the loyal men and women
of the United States Armed Services

We all commit ourselves to types of service
  devoted to maintain what we esteem
and with the talents that our lives are furnished
  apply our means to satisfy our needs.

And in the circumstances where we live
  we aim our interests toward what we intend
to balance what we get with what we give
  through the consent of fellow citizens.

But there are some who willingly consign
  to discipline and strict severity
and choose to put their own lives on the line,
  protecting others' ease and liberty.

Salute and cheer the Nation's noble soldiers.
God bless them for their courage, strength and honor.

*1861*

# *April 12-13*

Walt Whitman strolled amongst all those he loved,
   the throngs of people teeming in the streets,
and at the peak of all that had been done,
   he saw the endless possibilities.

Manhattan is an overflowing cup,
   a wash of life that surges through the streets,
and he could see the level rising up
   with the confluence of activities.

And buoyantly he swam through merry life,
   immersed within humanity's embrace
and yearned to understand the passers-by
   — each individual's distinguished way.

Each moment an arrival from the past,
   each life a story in the city's book,
with singing voices in the moving mass
   and portraits framed within the glancing look.

He heard the tapping of the carpenters
   that framed the spaces with the upright boards
and then enclosed the private corridors
   with finished work of snug and well fit doors.

And through the day he felt the city build,
   arising on the mass accomplishments
with intermeshing cogs of turning wheels
   that rested nightly in each residence.

The masts were standing at the harbor's docks,
   the hulls were weathered with the rimes of sea,
the stevedores were heaving heavy stocks
   while sailors were refreshed on their shore leave.

And as the ships were all securely moored
  the loads would hoist from hulls to circulate,
propelling commerce through the shops and stores
  with wares and goods the town would make and trade.

The barges on the Hudson brought produce,
  the apples from the orchards rolled downstream
and every item that was put to use
  was hauled on wheels with locomotive steam.

And each idea of ingenuity
  from cultivation of the turning ground
to fabrications of the industries
  was passing through the workings of this town.

The tools were made to satisfy demands
  as each accomplishment brought higher aims
as people broaden what they understand,
  communicating through their skills and trades.

Each job makes statements that become firm fact,
   informing with the services applied,
a satisfaction for what had been lacked,
   fulfilling work and workers as required.

And in the grandeur of this conversation
   demands and answers turned to broad exchange
involving all the city's population
   with other markets at a global range.

And in the hustle of the bustling town
   Walt Whitman relished all the energy,
absorbing every single sight and sound
   through the excitement of prosperity.

The streets were packed with people on the move,
   an intermeshing of the divers lives,
each alternating step of pays and dues
   with goods for trade and services to ply.

And quietly Walt stood off to the side
   to jot the notes of all he heard and saw,
composing articles for printers' type
   to circulate from the newspaper stalls.

Evoking characters that he described,
   portraying the events upon the page,
each reader witnessing what had transpired
   articulated through what Walt conveyed.

He noted hidden curiosities,
   informed of issues of the politics,
and celebrated common dignity
   in lines he wrote for public benefit.

As Emerson upon his lecture tours,
   a visionary orator and sage,
Walt aimed to reach each person in the world
   with the illumination of each phrase.

Acknowledging each individual
   with rhapsodies of lettered liberty,
he scripted what he found remarkable
   on grassy leaves of his sweet poetry.

Each statement is a stem of growing life,
   all similar yet each in its own way
arising from its roots to touch the light
   and flourishing upon the open page.

Each leaf conducts the music's instruments
   with subtle timber playing pitch and tone
with arias and sweet divertissements
   composed into the corresponding whole.

He rode the omnibuses through the streets
   — the *Broadway, Knickerbocker, Yellowbird*,
the moving rooms with spectacles to see
   where myriads of passages converge.

The buses always follow the same lines
   of measured schedules and a strict routine
but New York City changes all the time
   and every moment is a different scene.

The rolling intersections charge a fare
   and offer seats that move from place to place
and shrink the distances from here to there
   as motion is where trains and buses stay.

The people and the city are the same
   while loading and unloading at each stop.
Activity is how all is sustained —
   the whirling balance of the spinning top.

And Whitman stood beside the driver's seat
   with stops and starts made with a shout and bell
and listened through the intervals between
   to stories that the drivers loved to tell.

And riding buses up and down the streets
   he knew there was no single destination.
All destiny is an activity,
   the only goal is for perpetuation.

And every story opens a new world
   and each perspective gives a different view
and the distinctions can be seen and heard
   as every moment is completely new.

There is a world of wonder in each life
   and every touch is a discovery.
Walt played the strings of phrases he would write.
   The city was the music he would sing.

Museums would transport him back in time
   and in each book he read attentively
he journeyed through the fields of lively lines
   and on the move was where he loved to be.

And every book was like an omnibus
   where he could sit upon an open seat
and meet the people of the populace
   while gamboling through the revolving scenes.

Then after riding to the evening
   he hopped off-board close to the Bowery
near where he had a ticket for a seat
   at that night's opera on Fourteenth Street.

Each theater was filled with memories
   of shows that he would frequently attend
with local actors and celebrities
   for entertainment and extravagance.

But more than just a spectacle for show,
   the theater and opera enrich,
providing people who enjoy to go
   both cultured substance and embellishments.

The open doors drew from the crowded streets
    with the announcement of performance time
and tickets were then sold to fill the seats
    with people waiting eagerly outside.

Each playhouse had a permanent address
    where different acting troupes came marching through
and brought to life their own performances
    for local audiences to review.

And what before was but an empty stage
    was dressed for setting of the scenery
and actors rolled into the parts they played
    to bring to life a world of artistry.

But Whitman saw more than a simple show,
    he saw a broadening experience,
the lessons learned from tragedies and woes
    that balanced comedy's lightheartedness.

Each new performance set upon the stage
   and new arrangements of the opera
provided people with a civic place
   for commonwealth of shared euphoria.

And in the richness of each new production
   the audience could visit a new land,
transported through the musical conduction
   for new experience to understand.

And from the show set to perform that night
   inside the town's Academy of Music,
Walt was prepared for rapture and delight
   with inspiration of profound amusement.

Once in, then Walt would carefully inspect
   the balconies for well-known city leaders
who sat in upper tiers with Presidents,
   yet Walt felt best amongst the common people.

And as musicians tuned their instruments
    the crowd of people shuffled to their seats
and turned their lives to face astonishment
    anticipating what they'd hear and see.

When the conductor walked out on the floor
    he found a welcome of a warm applause
and straightened all the papers of the score
    and then there was the gloaming of the pause.

He signaled the musicians with a nod
    and not a single person said a word
then the conductor raised up his baton
    releasing passions of the overture.

The themes were heard in sequenced summary
    with tonic notes that the musicians played
and everyone was in rapt reverie
    when the red curtain lifted from the stage.

And through the window of the scenery
   the stage became a place for a new dawn
refreshed with breezes of sweet melodies
   with the enchanting story told in song.

The artfully unfolding of the tale
   excited the refreshment of each sense
where what was seen upon the stage was felt
   as music poured over the audience.

The living characters sang glowingly
   so even arguments were beautiful
and all the voices chimed in harmony
   and life was noted as remarkable.

And the grand opera explored the themes
   that touched upon the characters of life
in circumstances of society
   from tests of torment to the sweet delights.

The chorus with the volume of the cast
   resounded as the audience cohered
and soaring voices of the arias
   lifted the spirits through the atmosphere.

And as performances draw in the crowd
   conveying people to another place
in the attention to the sights and sounds
   a new world can unfold upon the stage.

Performance arts do more than entertain
   and have more substance than a fantasy,
the theaters let people congregate
   where individuals share empathy.

And with the operas that are performed
   with talent, skill and polished artistry
there is a commonality informed
   of individuals in unity.

And when the grand finale drew to close
    and the conductor's arms came to a rest
all the attendees for the evening's show
    erupted with a fresh exuberance.

And with applause and hollered curtain calls
    the crowd made their appreciation clear
with clattering ovations in the hall
    that is sweet music to the artists' ears.

Then Whitman walked back out into the night
    beneath the twinkling of the lofty stars
and had a sense of tension cinching tight
    and heard of declaration of a war.

The paperboys were running through the streets
    although the hour was long beyond midnight
and as their arms were waving printed sheets
    he heard the voices, "Extra! Extra!" cry.

Walt Whitman bought one of the papers then
   and stood amazed as he began to read —
Fort Sumter was bombarded at Charleston
   as Southern states were vying to secede.

And underneath a street lamp's glowing light
   Walt Whitman read the newspaper out loud
with shocking news that was announced that night
   as people on the block gathered around.

The rebels fired upon the Nation's flag,
   the emblem of the People's Liberty.
The Nation would be sadly split in half
   with cleaving hatred and hostility.

# Bull Run

Society arises through exchange
   with statements and responses alternating
and there are countless types and endless ways
   for people to conduct a conversation.

There is an affirmation in engagement,
   a thoughtful touch of warmly felt attention,
a repartee of casual conflation
   conforming with the manners of convention.

And every conversation lends invention,
   the give and take exchanged between perspectives,
with the distinctions from what is intended
   received with the allowance of acceptance.

It is the trade of feelings and ideas
　　that balance customs with the novelty
in ways the social graces may forgive
　　for ventures that contest propriety.

Sometimes eruptions of the wild dissensions
　　are quelled with facts that cannot be reputed
but there are always differing opinions
　　that never settle as they are disputed.

And there are lessons that are sorely learned
　　to broaden minds beyond self-serving needs
where understanding and respect is earned
　　to manage systems more expansively.

And every new development and growth
　　requires the pain of sacrifice and loss,
a reckoning between the high and low
　　as every gain is balanced with a cost.

And as attentive students learn in class
   they must endure and bear the growing pains,
improving on the lessons of the past
   so what is gained may wisely be sustained.

And as the conversations build in size
   through interactions of society,
the ideas circulate on busy lines
   of trade and commerce and new industry.

But then the Nation had to face the threat
   from the abominable institution
of slavery's infernal wickedness
   that compromised the Nation's Constitution.

The Founders staked their lives on the decree
   Declaring all men are created equal
with Independence from all tyranny
   as Liberty was granted to the People.

The number of the slave owners was small,
   a fraction of the people in the South
and of the population overall,
    they added to a nominal amount.

How were they able to exert control
   with lies of a superiority
and make the new Republic foil and spoil
    with fallacies of aristocracy?

And as the tension mounted through the years
   with pleads to conscience and humanity
the slave owners perversely would not yield
    to any sense of grace and decency.

When Lincoln was elected President,
   before he had been sworn in for his term,
secessionists seized mints and battlements
    and Southern loyalty swerved in a turn.

The rebels thought they had the upper hand
   with cotton as the economic king
and with a backwoodsman as President
   the ship of the Republic would soon sink.

Secessionists seized Federal armaments
   reserved below the Mason Dixon line
and rebels forming the confederates
   were passionate for a secession fight.

With no respect for the new President
   they felt the time was right to break away
convinced that Mr. Lincoln would submit
   and the United States would fray and fade.

But Unionists were not without their pluck
   and many had anticipated war.
With slavery as a confounded crutch
   the rebels had a weak and faulty core.

The Northern states were building industry
  with steam from boilers driving the machines,
developing with ingenuity
  for evolution of posterity.


Secession could not possibly succeed.
  The South could not maintain prosperity.
No human can be held as property.
  There is no liberty with slavery.


And isolated with their current means,
  the Southern states had no chance to endure,
relying on one sole commodity
  and weakened by not doing their own work.


The Union troops swelled with the volunteers.
  They thought the fight would end in a few months
and that the Union Army was prepared
  to march straight to the Southern capital.

The Nation's argument of slavery
   had rankled since the states had been devised.
The true integrity of liberty
   in founding principles was compromised.

Despite debate and rationality,
   the oligarchs of slaves refused to budge
and with the mounting of hostility
   the next laws would be writ in tears and blood.

And as communication is exchange
   this conversation flared with argument
and building with both bitterness and rage
   the interaction drove to violence.

And disagreeing on the civil grounds
   the speech began to build with martial means
and what is spoken from the cannon's mouth
   are roars of devastating tragedy.

Spectators gathered at the 1$^{st}$ Bull Run
   expecting to see a conclusive bout,
then Union ranks would march onto Richmond
   and the secession would be quickly trounced.

And in July on a hot summer day
   the battle pitched upon the grassy field
with lines of soldiered ranks in blue and grey
   while people watched from the surrounding hills.

The blazing fury of the battle front
   was burning in a fearsome parity
and then the fight's direction at Bull Run
   looked hopeful for a Union victory.

The column on the right had pushed with force
   and overwhelmed entrenchments like a flood.
The tide of Union blue pressed on the shore
   and drove the rebels back into the woods.

But with investments of the forward gain
  the column then was left out in the field,
a target within rebel cannon range
  for deadly enfilades from top a hill.


The rebel marksmen fired from distant trees
  as Union soldiers waited for support
and they were picked off as the rebels pleased
  and lost the surge of their momentous force.


The ammunition of the batteries
  had been exhausted with the forward charge
and without guns of the artillery
  they only had the infantry's small arms.


Then the reserves were never set to march
  and Jackson posted with his rebel ranks
and stood like a stone wall to stop the charge
  and rebel cavalry attacked the flanks.

Then rebels yelled a fiery countercharge
    with Johnston's army from the Shenandoah
that struck the Union flank with an alarm
    and scuttled in a fray the Union soldiers.

The Union soldiers fought to hold the ground
    but rebel reinforcements struck their side
and Union forces could not pivot round
    to fight the charge by forming a new line.

So Johnston's army drove straight through the flank
    and charging down from Shenandoah hills,
they ripped into the Union Army ranks
    and scattered Union soldiers on the field.

Commanders tried to organize the men
    but they were in the chaos of a storm
and in the clamor and disordered din
    the ranks of companies would not reform.

Spectators on the hills began to run,
   the soldiers scrambled to surrounding woods
and as the fighting on the field was done
   the footing of the rebels firmly stood.

Then heavy clouds covered the summer sky
   and weepy, drizzly rain began to fall
and there was dire concern and frenzied fright
   the rebels might then charge the Capital.

The hope that the dispute might end that day
   was shattered when the battle had been lost
and then the grisly war began to rage
   in wages paid with mortifying costs.

The soldiers clambered back to Washington.
   They had no camp but people gave them food.
Most had to sleep that night out in the rain
   and people were bewildered and confused.

There was no question of the sad defeat
   and many thought they should withdraw the fight,
relent to let the Southern states secede
   and many said that Lincoln should resign.

Yet the new President was confident
   and answered bickering with rationale,
responding to hardship with diligence
   to keep the focus of the Capitol.

He listened to the reasoning opinions,
   dissented to the nattering distortions,
and ordering the matters of attention
   he organized the National resources.

He pushed ahead to blockade Southern ports.
   The cotton was the South's exclusive means
and if the South could not sell their export
   they couldn't buy supplies their troops would need.

The Union had developed industry
    and transportation for required supplies,
if they could keep a strong economy
    they'd persevere in an extended fight.

And in the storm of turbulence at sea
    the President stood firm upon the helm
and would not waver from his certainty
    — the Union of the Nation would be held.

*1862*

# *Fredericksburg*

For forty years Walt Whitman watched parades
  with soldiers marching through the city streets
with celebrations of abundant days
  in comfort of security and peace.

At five he had attended one event
  — the building of a public library.
The corner stone was set by Lafayette
  who picked up Walt and hugged him to his breast.

And with the city's glorious parades
  with joyful music from the marching bands,
the people lined the streets as banners waved
  for holidays observed across the land.

In strength and cadence of their discipline
  the soldiers marched in polished unity
with solemn oaths to fight in the defense
  of all the people's gift of liberty.

The crowds would gather in uplifting cheer
  for life and happiness each one pursued
and proudly raised up high throughout the year
  the stars and stripes that waved red, white and blue.

But then the soldiers marched in their platoons
  and carried what the armories had stored
and then the ranks of the enlisted troops
  were marching off into the fires of war.

The people cheered their loyal warriors
  and honored soldiers for their sacrifice
— courageous regulars and volunteers
  who willingly put their lives on the line.

And Walt was cheering for the righteous cause.
  He'd taken his own stand on slavery
and for this he had been fired from his job
  as he opposed the inhumanity.

And he had seen his younger brother George
  sign up and join for liberty's defense
and proudly watched him march into the war
  to take a stand for truth and righteousness.

His brother joined after the 1$^{st}$ Bull Run
  and had been fighting fiercely for a year
— for three months with a Brooklyn regiment
  and then he joined the New York Volunteers.

Then reading of the loss at Fredericksburg
  Walt was distressed to see his brother's name
in a long list of those who were injured
  with thousands of the soldiers who were slain.

The battle had been a catastrophe.
   The Union had by far the stronger force
and General Burnside tried to gain on Lee
   but had been stuck at Rappahannock's shore.

They had expected to meet engineers
   with the pontoons they needed for a bridge
but the equipment had not be transferred
   and they were held up at the water's edge.

And while they waited, rebels built in force
   and dug into the hills above the town
and by the time they crossed the river's course
   they were in the gunsights from all around.

There was a narrow field by Fredericksburg
   the Union Army tried to storm across
but each battalion that charged in their turn
   was decimated at a total loss.

Their numbers were an overwhelming force
   if they could only reach the rebel line
but every charging wave that had been formed
   was cut to pieces viciously each time.

And as they faced the horrors of the war,
   the courage of the soldiers would not yield,
although each time they were lined up to charge
   they looked through smoke into a killing field.

And murder raged through the entire day
   as each wave smashed into a wall of lead.
The opportunity had passed away
   and the sad field was covered with the dead.

And Whitman sat in his peaceful repose
   and through the window saw the busy street
and from the comforts of his modest home
   the life around was flowing easily.

He wrote for papers to report the war.
    He knew the matters of the State were dire
but sometimes wondered if the people cared
    that half of the Republic was on fire.

The people have to carry on with life,
    society cannot shut down to grieve
but all around them was a ring of fire
    that would rush to consume complacency.

They walked with ease and safety through the streets.
    The markets were all stocked with what they need.
Life does require responsibility
    but they had no concern of tyranny.

Their homes and towns could be bombarded too.
    Their livelihoods could be robbed and destroyed.
The proud Republic that they constitute
    could crumble into savagery and spoils.

The Nation's crisis had split them in half
  and threatened every person's liberty.
They reached the point where there's no turning back.
  They had to break the bonds of slavery.

So Whitman then began to travel south
  to try to find and help his brother George.
The army had been camping at Falmouth
  from what he had been reading in reports.

Arriving in Virginia on the train
  the locomotive slowed in the approach
and Whitman saw in the cold, winter day
  a city made of tents in ordered rows.

The soldiers huddled round the scattered fires
  and breathed their steamy breath into their hands
and underneath the blue and icy sky
  they stomped their boots upon the frozen land.

Some companies were drilling in a field
   and practiced the maneuvering platoons
and as another early grave was filled
   a squad fired muskets to sound the salute.

And Whitman found these seven gun salutes
   were frequently fired throughout every day
and every time he flinched because he knew
   another soldier was set in a grave.

And when Walt Whitman stepped off board the train
   he asked where the hospital could be found
and he could not forget the soldier's face
   whose countenance was heavy and profound.

The soldier still appeared to be a boy,
   he couldn't have been older than sixteen,
and carved a name onto a wooden board
   and turned to look at Whitman distantly.

His youthful face was flecked with mud and dirt
   and Walt could not imagine where he'd been
but from the writings of the war reports
   Walt cringed to think what the young man had seen.

The soldier looked up at the bearded man
   across the chasms oceans cannot fill
and lifted up the jackknife in his hand
   and pointed to a mansion on a hill.

Then walking up the path that climbed the slope
   Walt Whitman saw more boards with whittled names
that rose upon the mansion's gentle knoll
   to mark the rows and lines of the fresh graves.

Then yards away he saw the mansion's porch
   with columns standing with the Union Flag
and not far from the entrance's grand doors
   there was a heaping mound of bloody rags.

But walking closer Whitman could then see
   the pile he saw was not what he had thought
but amputated arms, hands, legs and feet
   that casualties of war had sadly lost.

And then a surgeon stepped out of the doors
   and tossed another arm onto the pile
that tumbled flopping down the heap of gore
   and Whitman froze with the unnerving sight.

The surgeon glared at Whitman standing stunned
   and quickly turned to get back to his work,
he had no time to dwell upon the glum
   there were too many soldiers gravely hurt.

Walt Whitman would not dare to back away,
   he had to face the terror of the war
and offered what he could in his own way
   and walked straight through the hospital's front doors.

The soldiers were the Union's sacrifice
   on the foundations of life's liberty
and valiantly the soldiers risked their lives
   and Walt would not forsake them in their need.

He dressed the wounds.  He comforted the grief.
   He gave compassion to the bleak and grim.
Some in convulsions grabbed his passing sleeve
   and he would sit for hours to comfort them.

He found his brother to his great relief.
   George had been injured but the wound was slight
and he had made a full recovery
   and was resolved to get back in the fight.

Then Whitman travelled up to Washington
   with soldiers who were carried and transferred
upon a steamship of the government
   and helped the injured as a volunteer.

He found a job as an official clerk
   to cover his expenses and his bills
and then fulfilling his position's work
   he donated his time at hospitals.

*1863*

# Chancellorsville

Walt Whitman lodged at a small boarding house
    and volunteered at army hospitals
and many buildings of the Capital
    were filled with soldiers throughout Washington.

The streets were rivers of blue uniforms
    with soldiers posted at surrounding forts
and just the sick and injured in the wards
    doubled the population through the war.

And thousands of the beds were lined in rows
    with sick and injured soldiers from the front
who had been suffering the battle blows
    from dysentery as much as from the guns.

Then General Burnside was relieved command
  after the Fredericksburg catastrophe.
Joe Hooker then worked to improve the camps
  to boost the soldiers' spirit with his lead.

Much of the time the soldiers had to wait
  with sputtered skirmishes at picket lines
but Hooker kept them focused and engaged
  in drills with purpose for a clear design.

Refreshment of supplies and nourishment
  had raised morale within the infantry,
assuring soldiers that the leadership
  prepared the way for Union victories.

The rebels were determined and entrenched
  and Hooker had to beat Robert E. Lee
to crush the rebel army's battlements
  and end the Civil War decisively.

But when the Union Army moved to fight
   to try to pry the rebels from their holes
the army could not concentrate to strike
   and leave the Nation's Capital exposed.

So blocking Lee from charging Washington
   Joe Hooker lead the troops in his command
to find a way to organize the men
   and break through the confederate's defense.

And patiently the General built the strength,
   developing a new strategic plan
and drilled the corps of army infantry
   to galvanize each soldier's confidence.

In Washington, Walt worked in hospitals
   and volunteered wherever there was need
and knew the soldiers were responsible
   for the defense of precious liberty.

The soldiers bore the brunt of injury
    yet none complained or moaned about their woes.
They were the country's brave nobility
    with courage to confront oppressive foes.

Inside the Patent Office was a ward
    with cots arranged to fill the second floor.
The halls were lined with locked display, glass doors
    with space appropriated for the war.

Behind the glass were modeled miniatures
    of the inventions that were patented,
ingenious tools that had been registered
    and filled the Patent Office cabinets.

And each design accomplished certain jobs
    and each was made to satisfy demands
and the still models set above the cots
    of agonizing lines of injured men.

And gazing at inventions on display
  Walt pondered the potential of each man,
each in possession of distinctive traits
  with different talents of their minds and hands.

And in the commerce of congruent lives
  through all the ways people communicate
with every loss another wonder dies
  — the miracles that tragedies erase.

Humanity must scramble to create
  supports to shore against collapse and fall
but then in turn these new inventions make
  more problems that are needed to be solved.

And all the multitudes of human life
  agree that problems must be overcome
but in the struggle to do what is right
  it seems more horrible things must be done.

Walt had to hold the soldiers in restraint
   when the infection of gangrene was dire
and then the surgeon sawed to amputate
   in hopes the dropping limb would save a life.

Then Whitman heard announcements of the need
   for volunteers to work upon the wharf.
The river boats were filled with casualties
   and they were set to dock soon after dark.

At 8 they carried stretchers from the boats
   and soldiers had to lie upon the ground
and then the stormy clouds began to roll
   and heavy rain began to thunder down.

The Chancellorsville campaign had fell apart
   and Lee had countered Hooker's planned attack
and found soft spots in Hooker's forward march
   and heavy losses drove the Union back.

The soldiers on the wharf laid in the rain
    while workers hustled to unload the boats
so they could promptly sail back down again
    to try to staunch the gushing flow of blood.

And still none of the soldiers would complain
    while waiting for an open ambulance,
enduring the discomfort and the pain
    with temperance and stout resilience.

Yet Whitman grieved at the horrendous sight
    of mangled lives with their horrific wounds
and struggled to assist the soldiers' plight
    and move them to the hospitals' safe rooms.

And soldiers from both of the conflict's sides
    were then at peace together as they came
and clamping down to keep them all alive
    the surgeons treated all of them the same.

There was no animosity or shame,
   the soldiers were the victims of the fight.
It was the monstrous war that was to blame
   and surgeons worked to save each soldier's life.

A thousand soldiers would arrive each day
   and Whitman worked with others tirelessly
in hopes that every injured life was saved
   while weeping poems on blood splattered leaves.

# Gettysburg

As Whitman worked in the hospital wards
   he recognized the different ways to help,
the sanitation and the messy work
   to lift the soldiers' spirits and their health.

Walt found the simple things the soldiers need
   were little gifts that would improve their moods,
a simple thought to ease the misery
   and spark a smile to lift the heavy gloom.

He paid for postage and bought envelopes
   so soldiers could send letters to their homes
and other soldiers who were all alone
   enjoyed when Walt recited Homer's poems.

He'd bring them homemade food and store bought candy
   to help to mollify their sense of loss
and from his wallet gave them his own money
   and shared the hope that any good news brought.

The soldiers who had fought at Chancellorsville
   were baffled by the Federal defeat.
They thought a triumph was inevitable
   and that the rebels would be soundly beat.

But even with the dour discouragement
   none of the soldiers in the wards complained
and they resisted any bitterness
   their sacrifices may have been in vain.

Then General Lee decided to advance
   and march into the Pennsylvanian hills
and with the Southern states' armed regiments
   he aimed to charge into the Capital.

Lee's army only faced militias
   that scattered from the overwhelming force,
and like a monstrous pandemonium,
   the rebels moved upon a plotting course.

The Union scouts set out to track the path
   of trampled ground and ruts of wagon wheels
to follow movements of the planned attack
   to squarely meet upon the battlefield.

And by the quiet farms at Gettysburg
   some Union troops entrenched outside of town
to stop the progress of the rebel surge
   as the secession force built up around.

Then the Potomac Army moved in place
   upon the ridge of Cemetery Hill
while forces at the outskirts slowed the pace
   of rebel columns marching to the field.

Then the front line withdrew up to the ridge
   that the confederates could not march past
and then the Union soldiers all dug in
   and rebel forces mounted for attack.

The massive troop maneuvers through the day
   were carried on into the dusky light
and with the lines of troops set into place
   both of the armies settled for the night.

And Union soldiers looking out below
   could see the hostile rebel force's span
with countless campfires flaring with bellows
   of angry voices singing "Dixie's Land".

As Lincoln stood he faced the harsh abuse
   and held the helm in the ferocious storm
and General Meade and his Potomac troops
   had clearly drawn the line and said, "No more!"

In Washington on the Fourth of July
   Walt Whitman walked along the avenues,
despite the war and agonizing trials
   he felt the sense of a refreshing mood.

He heard the music of a marching band
   with rolling drums and notes of polished brass
with banners soaring over every span
   and wave on wave of the bright Union Flags.

Between the rounds of army hospitals
   Walt Whitman paused to cheer the proud parade
and stood along with crowds in Washington
   for celebrating Independence Day.

But as he watched the celebrations pass
   he thought of prices loyal soldiers pay
who take the brunt to hold the Union fast
   securing independence every day.

And when the festive fair had settled down
   after the passing of the promenade
there was a somber quiet all around
   and Walt thought of the soldiers in their pain.

After the crowds returned to their routines
   from gathering to celebrate in bliss
Walt strolled to the news office down the street
   to look for any posted bulletins.

Then Whitman read the banner joyfully,
   the course of war had made an epic turn
with a decisive Union victory
   — the rebel charge was crushed at Gettysburg.

So Walt went to the local general store
   and bought a case of bottled berry syrup
and made his rounds to soldiers in the wards
   with sweets to drink and joyful news to cheer them.

With water mixed with syrup in their cups
    and savoring the glorious report,
the spirits of the soldiers were lit up
    with hope for a conclusion of the war.

Then through the afternoon and into dusk
    they laughed and sang the songs they loved to sing,
then suddenly fell quiet with a hush
    and heard the bells outside begin to ring.

*1864*

# At the Rapidan

The busy work of war can seem absurd
  by building barricades soon left behind
then carefully constructing what will burn
  as vessels bravely launch into the fire.

And near the camp along the Rapidan
  the soldiers chopped to fell the forest trees
and sawed the boards according to a plan
  to build another structure dutifully.

But this was no defensive palisade
  or structure for a surgeon's hospital,
it was a hall that would accommodate
  the 2$^{nd}$ Army Corps officers' ball.

And wives and sweethearts travelled in by train
  at a safe distance from any attack
and elegantly waltzed in promenade
  with decorations of the Union Flags.

Outside, a grandstand also had been made
  with fresh pine planks that had been sanded smooth
and all the soldiers lined up the next day
  and marched past in their ranks for the review.

The war continued ruthlessly to rage
  without clear sight of any peaceful end
and there were many soldiers on parade
  the wives and sweethearts would not see again.

And from the icy, February night
  then following through the cold winter day
a ceremony for brave sacrifice
  was ordered and respectfully displayed.

And at Culpepper twenty miles away
  Walt Whitman helped the soldiers near the front
with Brooklyn's own proud 14th in array
  through the hardships of the cold, winter months.

They guarded what had been a rendezvous
  for the secession troops two years before,
an intersection of important routes
  for the maneuvers of the shifting war.

They kept their guard alertly at the posts,
  their lives were on the line all night and day,
and skirmishes would flare between the foes
  but much of war is a dull, numbing wait.

They did not have the grandeur of a ball,
  yet soldiers still had means to entertain
and held their own theater in a hall
  with skits and music that they loved to play.

And Walt enjoyed attending every show
   and often turned to look into the crowd
to see the youthful soldiers' faces glow
   intent, intelligent, strong, brave and proud.

Then there was word in camp that they would move
   and restlessness turned to uncertainty.
They craved for something purposeful to do
   but rumors also stirred anxiety.

When the machines of war begin to turn
   it is a fierce and mighty sight to see
and no one knows this more than those who serve
   as soldiers in the Army's infantry.

And in the middle of the chilly night
   Walt Whitman was awoken by the shouts
as the 14$^{th}$ set in their camp nearby
   was ordered to pack up and to move out.

And Whitman heard the shuffle as they packed
    as boots were marching in a strict cadence.
He crawled out of his spartan bivouac
    and rose into the open from his tent.

Then walking to the edge of the main road
    Walt watched a river uniformed in blue
and felt the powerful, momentous flow
    of the strong Union Army on the move.

And sometimes he heard soldiers humming songs
    or sometimes friendly laughter in the ranks
but as they marched before the light of dawn
    Walt never heard one murmur a complaint.

The $14^{th}$ packed up gear efficiently
    and after breaking camp the lines were formed
and in the order of each company
    each soldier made the solid Army Corps.

And the 14<sup>th</sup> then joined into the march,
   another unit in the column's strength,
with miles of soldiers marching in the dark
   in hopes and prayers to reach the victory.

And Whitman felt the States being renewed
   in such a way he'd never felt before
and of what all the Nation constitutes
   the liberty and law would be reborn.

And after issuing Emancipation
   for the abolishment of slavery,
the President made a new proclamation
   to grant secessionists an amnesty.

Then they could put an end to bloody war
   and stop the rife destruction mercifully
and equally from how they had been born
   develop means through their civility.

They needed to reach Richmond with the statement
  so forces set in various maneuvers
for some diverting tactical engagements
  that would allow the pamphlet's distribution.

But the elaborate plan soon fell apart
  and yet another hopeful light was snuffed.
It seemed there was no way to end the war
  entrenched so neither side would give or budge.

So General Grant was called to Washington
  and given the commission of command
to pound and pound and bring the hammer down
  and drive this hellish war unto its end.

*1865*

# *April 14-16*

1.

Walt Whitman stood beneath the lilac blooms
   in the bright ripeness of the April day
and read the paper and the joyful news
   of peace regained in the United States.

The *Evening Star* said that the President
   intended to accompany his wife
at a performance they planned to attend
   at Ford Theater later that same night.

And Whitman knew that Lincoln loved the plays,
   he'd seen him many times at theaters,
but thought the drama acted on the stage
   a silly masquerade of amateurs

compared to the role Lincoln had performed
to save the Nation from a hellish war.

2.
To save the Nation from a hellish war
    required a common, ordinary man
who built his fortitude and character
    by working hard through his development.

No stranger to the challenges in life,
    he struggled and he honestly achieved
abilities that he learned to apply
    with remedies of his sagacity.

And through the richness of experience
    he paid for hard won lessons on his own
providing for his own deliverance
    with values scratched out from his humble home.

And from the stock of common, hardy folk,
he was prepared to play uncommon roles.

3.

He was prepared to play uncommon roles
   and Whitman saw this from the very first
after he won at the election polls
   and showed resolve through all he had endured.

He knew that all men are created equal,
   this truth is certainly self-evident
and precious rights respected by the People
   must be protected by self-government.

The compromises that were made for years
   corrupted national integrity.
The Nation was a commonwealth of peers
   and the strong Union ended slavery.

No person is another's property.
And Lincoln took the stand for his beliefs.

4.

And Lincoln took the stand for his beliefs
   with anti-slavery Republicans
and won the vote with his integrity
   to end the teetering permissiveness.

A feudal evil had a clenching hold
   and threatened tearing the whole Nation down
and when diplomacy was blocked and foiled
   only infernal war could burn it out.

So desperate times demanded desperate measures,
   the Nation was impeded in its course.
They had to break dehumanizing fetters
   with grievous use of military force

defending the Republic's unity
as Lincoln took a stand for Liberty.

5.

As Lincoln took a stand for Liberty
   he was a man of moral principles
yet had a seasoned sensibility
   negotiating with the practical.

He raised a beacon for the high ideals
   and had a knowledge of the ways and means.
The allegories that his mind revealed
   showed myriads of possibilities.

And with the stories from his humble past
   to the complexities of politics,
he offered clarity that was exact
   as axioms of Euclid's *Elements*.

And as he stood with honest dignity
he luminated life with brilliancy.

6.

He luminated life with brilliancy
   that Whitman saw distinctly on Broadway
with a short visit to New York City
   before his first Inauguration Day.

For blocks the city had come to a halt
   and Lincoln gazed upon the gathered crowd
and all the boisterous bustling had stopped
   and something settled quietly profound.

And Lincoln stood in front of Astor House,
   a folk profoundness of the populace,
and viewing him from overhead the crowd
   Walt sat on top of a parked omnibus.

Then on the 16th Walt broke down to weep
with these fond thoughts and vivid memories.

7.

With these fond thoughts and vivid memories
   Walt read the news of the assassination.
The triumph of the Union victory
   was riddled with a tragic devastation.

Two days before he read what someone wrote
   of Lincoln planning to attend a play
and after one scene of the evening's show
   a hateful man took Lincoln's life away.

The President began his second term
   and there was so much more he could have done
with Liberty and Unity's return
   after the Civil War was finally won.

And all those poignant moments were renewed
each time Walt Whitman smelled the lilacs bloom.

## Acknowledgements

This book is based upon Walt Whitman's personal accounts of the Civil War that can be found in *Leaves of Grass* and *Specimen Days*. Some details of military events were informed by Bruce Catton's *The Army of the Potomac* Trilogy. In the chapter "At the Rapidan" – the 2nd Army Corps officers' ball and the attempt to spread amnesty proclamations to people in Richmond were based upon descriptions by Catton. Some details for the 1st Battle of Bull Run were based upon personal descriptions of Samuel J. English in his letter to his mother on July 24, 1861. Some details were also informed by Carl Sandburg's biography: *Abraham Lincoln*.

In the chapters "Bull Run" and "April 14-16" there are direct quotes from the Declaration of Independence. Both President Abraham Lincoln and Walt Whitman held the firm position that the Declaration of Independence is the foundational document of the United States of America.

The epigraph for the book is from the "Preface Note to 2nd Annex" of Walt Whitman's *Leaves of Grass*. It is one of the last statements written by Walt Whitman in his life.

For Walt Whitman's poetry and prose, the letter by Samuel J. English and the Declaration of Independence, I read from The Library of America volumes. For Bruce Catton, I read my father's Doubleday and Company, Inc. volumes (1962). For Carl Sandburg, I read my great-grandfather's Sangamon Edition from Charles Scribner's Sons (1944).

Garrett Buhl Robinson was born in 1971 and raised in Trussville, Alabama. In 1992, he jumped on a coal train at a switchyard in Irondale and travelled around the United States for a year. Since that time, he has lived at numerous locations while writing prolifically, studying intensely and supporting himself with odd jobs. He currently lives and works in New York City.

---

Some other books by Garrett Buhl Robinson

<u>Poetry</u>
Pilgrims
Ballet Lessons
Whispering Emily
Satires
The Nobody
City of Poems
A Man Who Lives in a Dream
Beauty beyond Reason
Martha

<u>Prose</u>
Zoë
Nunatak

Poet in the Park
In Humanity I see Grace, Beauty and Dignity.
www.PoetinthePark.com